Happy Doodle

HairDoodle
by Heather Tesch

Written and illustrated by Heather Tesch,
"HairDoodle by Heather Tesch" is an addictively fun and easy
way to reduce stress and boost creativity.

A Brain-Building and Calming
Coloring and Doodle Book
for Adults and Teens

Thank You!

Publishing a book has been a life-long dream of mine. Thank you to all of you who are supporting my dream by purchasing, giving, or receiving this book.

I hope "HairDoodle by Heather Tesch" brings fun, creativity, and hours of joy into your life or the life of someone you care about.

Sincerely,
Heather Tesch

Hair Doodle
By Heather Tesch

This book is dedicated to my mother,
Janie Tesch-Cassady,
who has always encouraged me to
draw and write. Her belief in my
talent has given me the confidence I
needed to make this book a reality.

Thanks Mom for not only passing
on your artistic genes but also
giving me wings to fly.

"SUCCESS IS NOT JUST WHAT
YOU ACCOMPLISH IN YOUR LIFE,
IT IS ABOUT WHAT YOU INSPIRE
OTHERS TO DO."

- FROM INSPIRE YOUR MIND

HairDoodle by Heather Tesch
was written and illustrated by Heather Tesch

Printed in the United States of America

First Printing, 2016

ISBN: 978-0998334806

Author photo by Samantha Mohr

Tesch Ink
1634 Old 41 Hwy
Suite 112 - 242
Kennesaw, GA 30152

HairDoodle.com
Facebook.com/HeatherTesch.TV

HairDoodle
by Heather Tesch

CONTENTS

A Brain-Building and Calming
Coloring and Doodle Book
for Adults and Teens

EVERY CHILD IS AN
ARTIST. THE PROBLEM IS
STAYING AN ARTIST
WHEN YOU GROW UP.

PABLO PICASSO

Hand-Drawn Illustrations

"IMPERFECTION IS BEAUTY"
MARILYN MONROE

Many coloring books today contain computer generated art. I have hand drawn each HairDoodle. My hand-drawn art will not have perfect symmetry and it will contain small imperfections. Some lines will wobble and some lines will be thicker than others. I believe imperfections make art more interesting. Art is about fun and creating something uniquely ours. Please remember this as you fill in the pages of this book. Don't worry about mistakes and imperfections, simply enjoy the process of doodling and coloring.

"I ALWAYS FIND BEAUTY IN THINGS THAT ARE ODD AND IMPERFECT - THEY ARE MUCH MORE INTERESTING."
MARC JACOBS

Introduction to HairDoodle
by Heather Tesch

"HairDoodle by Heather Tesch" is an addictively fun and easy way to reduce stress and boost creativity. It combines the therapeutic benefits of coloring with the brain-building benefits of doodling.

Bring each HairDoodle to life by filling the blank spaces with designs. Use my HairDoodle template as inspiration for your designs. Follow the patterns exactly, change them to your liking, or come up with your own designs. Don't worry about mistakes or imperfections. Doodling isn't about perfection it is about fun.

Most of the doodle patterns in this book are very simple. By putting several simple patterns together on the same page your completed HairDoodle will look deceptively complicated. Every pattern you add increases the complexity of your HairDoodle. As your HairDoodle grows more elaborate your satisfaction and sense of achievement should grow too.

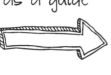 Use my HairDoodle Template as a guide

HairDoodle Template

 Fill the spaces with patterns

HairDoodle for you to complete

What You Will Need

1. This Book of HairDoodle Pages

2. Thin Black Permanent Marker

3. Colored Pencils

RED BLUE GREEN YELLOW PINK

COLORED PENCILS

ASTONISHING BENEFITS LINKED TO DOODLING AND COLORING

HairDoodle is not only fun, it is actually good for you in numerous ways! It combines the therapeutic benefits of coloring with the brain-building benefits of doodling. Neuroscientists and psychologists are now discovering that activities like HairDoodle are a great way to tune up our brains and improve our overall health.

Regular participation in an activity like HairDoodle has been scientifically proven to:

Enhance Memory
Improve Focus
Reduce Stress
Ignite Creativity
Expand Thinking
Boost Problem Solving
Keep Us Present
Reduce Depression
Increase Positive Emotions
Improve Immune System
Shorten Hospital Stays
Lower Pain Levels

Hmmm. Find all of this hard to believe? Read on.

HAIRDOODLE FOR YOUR HEALTH
THE SCIENCE BEHIND DOODLING

At this point some of you may want to get busy working on a HairDoodle. For those of you still skeptical or curious about the amazing health benefits associated with activities like HairDoodling, read on. Here are some of the findings from experts and researchers.

* Creative expression has a powerful impact on our emotional, mental, and even physical health.

In a paper published in the "American Journal Public Health", Heather L. Stuckey, DEd and Jeremy Nobel, MD, MPH, looked at more than 100 studies in the area of art and healing. They found that artistic expression can powerfully impact our health, well-being, and quality of life, stating that participation in artistic activities leads to "a variety of outcomes including a decrease in depressive symptoms, an increase in positive emotions, reduction in stress responses, and, in some cases, even improvements in immune system functioning"

* Creative art activities can decrease negative emotions and depression.

Stuckey and Nobel's paper points to several studies that showed patients with serious illnesses, such as cancer, who took part in creative art activities showed an overall improvement in their well-being, with a decrease in negative emotions and depression, and an increase in positive emotions. Some of those same studies showed a decrease in their level of pain.

* Making time for art can improve health and even renew energy

Researchers from the University of West England did a hospital study comparing the use and non-use of art intervention to improve patient health. They found that patients that received the art intervention were significantly more likely to have better vital signs, diminished stress hormones, and needed less medication to help them fall asleep.

A study at Northwestern Memorial Hospital, in Chicago, published in the "Journal of Pain Symptom Management" showed that even one hour of art activity significantly reduced pain symptoms in cancer patents. But that wasn't the only benefit. A surprising finding of this study was that patients reported feeling less tired and more energized after just one hour of art therapy.

* Doodling helps your concentration and memory.

An often sited British study by cognitive psychologist Jackie Andrade (School of Psychology, University of Plymouth, UK) shows that doodlers retain more information than non-doodlers. Her study found that doodling while working on other tasks can be beneficial - unlike most other dual task situations. Not only did doodlers in her study perform better on tasks, they also scored nearly 30% better on a surprise memory test.

*Doodle your problems away - or at least some of them.

Andrade also found that doodling takes our minds off of our problems and allows our subconscious mind to come up with a solution. She compares it to dreaming. "The same thing can happen when sleeping. You spend all day trying to solve a problem without success, only to wake up in the morning thinking 'Aha! That's the answer.'"

*Creative activities such as doodling and coloring can help generate ideas.

Philosophy professor at City University of New York Graduate Center, Jesse Prinz, studies doodling. Similarly to what Andrade found, Prinz says taking part in creative activities "makes us more creative by opening us up to more exploratory avenues of thought." "If you spend half an hour doing something creative, when someone gives you a problem you will think about it in fresh ways."

*Doodling keeps you in the present moment.

Prinz, also says that doodling prevents our mind from wandering and keeps us receptive to information by putting us in a state of what he calls "pure listening".

* Doodling can expand creativity.

Professional sculptor and painter Lorina Capitulo of North Babylon, New York credits doodling with unlocking and expanding her creativity. She claims doodling opened new avenues of artistic expression when she had been feeling stuck.

* Doodling and coloring reduces stress.

Spramani Elaun, a child art expert and art therapist says that creative activities like doodling and coloring cause cognitive responses that effect our emotions and promote relaxation. She says that when we become focused on these activities the electrical activity in our brain changes. Our minds calm down and stresses fade away.

SO MUCH FOR THE OUT-DATED THINKING
THAT DOODLING IS SIMPLY GOOFING OFF!

THROUGH CREATIVITY AND IMAGINATION, WE FIND OUR IDENTITY AND OUR RESERVOIR OF HEALING. THE MORE WE UNDERSTAND THE RELATIONSHIP BETWEEN CREATIVE EXPRESSION AND HEALING, THE MORE WE WILL DISCOVER THE HEALING POWER OF THE ARTS.

THE CONNECTION BETWEEN ART, HEALING, AND PUBLIC HEALTH: A REVIEW OF CURRENT LITERATURE
HEATHER L. STUCKEY, DED AND JEREMY NOBEL, MD, MPH

Clearly, regular participation in artistic activities like HairDoodling can greatly improve our health and well-being.

Setting time aside for doodling or similar activities should be as important as eating healthy and exercising.
Besides, when it comes to things we should do to stay healthy, doodling is probably the easiest and most fun.

"ART IS A CONSTANT AGENT OF TRANSFORMATION AND IS INDEED THE SOUL'S DRIVE TO HEALTH."

-CATHY MALCHIODI, THE SOUL'S PALETTE, DRAWINGS ON ART'S TRANSFORMATIVE POWERS FOR HEALTH AND WELL-BEING

KENDRA

I've put extra pages between HairDoodles so you don't have to worry about markers leaking through to another HairDoodle.

Use these extra pages to doodle, practice doodle patterns, come up with new doodle patterns, test colors, and be creative - but please use a pencil instead of a marker.

HALEY

18

Even though there is no right or wrong way to doodle, you may find it helpful to practice drawing some patterns before you add them to a HairDoodle. Use a pencil to practice those doodle patterns here.

KIMBERLY

22

Need a lift? Doodle.
Doodling reduces depression and increases positive emotions.
Use a pencil and give these gals at the HairDoodle Salon
some uplifting hairdos.

EBONY

26

GET YOUR CREATIVE JUICES FLOWING.
DOODLING BOOSTS CREATIVITY.

Look around you for patterns. Do you see anything that inspires you to come up with a new doodle pattern? Use a pencil to jot down your pattern ideas here.

JANIE

Get creative with some crazy hairdos.
Use a colored pencil or crayon and give these gals some style.

I call this Hairdo
a Poodle Doodle

SHERRY

34

THE DESIRE TO CREATE IS
ONE OF THE DEEPEST
YEARNINGS OF THE HUMAN
SOUL.

ELDER UCHTDORF

CREATIVITY IS INVENTING,
EXPERIMENTING, GROWING,
TAKING RISKS, BREAKING
RULES, MAKING MISTAKES,
AND HAVING FUN.

MARY LOU COOK

WEATHER GIRL   38

HAIRDOODLE SALON

These clients at the HairDoodle Salon want fancy new 'dos.

SEDONA

42

"OFTEN THE FEAR OF NOT KNOWING WHAT TO DO OR THE FEAR OF DOING SOMETHING WRONG STOPS US IN OUR TRACKS AND KEEPS US FROM STARTING. IF WE CAN LET GO OF THIS FEAR, WE OPEN OURSELVES UP TO A MUCH LARGER WORLD OF EXPRESSION, A WORLD WHERE ANYTHING IS POSSIBLE."

FLORA BOWLEY
BRAVE INTUITIVE PAINTING
AN ART JOURNAL FOR LIVING CREATIVELY

DAVIE

46

Quickly page through a magazine and search for patterns and shapes that inspire you to create new doodle patterns. Draw those patterns here.

PAULA

50

HAIRDOODLE SALON

You are a stylist at the HairDoodle salon. These clients are looking for some fun, fresh, and colorful styles. Use colored pencils and style away.

TERI

54

Use a pencil to practice doodle patterns here.

MARY LEE

58

HAIRDOODLE SALON

ROBIN

62

DOODLING WORKS YOUR CREATIVE MUSCLES.

One of the great things about doodling is that it removes our self imposed barriers of how things must be done. Because there are no right or wrong ways to doodle, doodling frees our mind and allows us to create fearlessly.

Challenge yourself to doodle for at least a few minutes each day and see how your mind flourishes. You will be surprised to discover that you will not only become more creative as an artist, you will actually become more creative in all areas of your life.

CRYSTAL

CREATIVITY IS
INTELLIGENCE HAVING FUN.
ALBERT EINSTEIN

TO LIVE A CREATIVE LIFE
WE MUST LOSE OUR FEAR
OF BEING WRONG.
JOSEPH CHILTON PEARCE

BETTY

HAIRDOODLE SALON

These clients are looking for some fancy updos.

TRACY

Use a pencil and try to come up with your own doodle patterns.

CHRISTI

JOELLE

82

HAIRDOODLE SALON

LAURA

TRUE INTELLIGENCE
OPERATES SILENTLY.
STILLNESS IS WHERE
CREATIVITY AND
SOLUTIONS TO PROBLEMS
ARE FOUND.

REGINA MALABAGO

YOU CAN'T USE UP
CREATIVITY. THE MORE
YOU USE, THE MORE YOU
HAVE.

MAYA ANGELOU

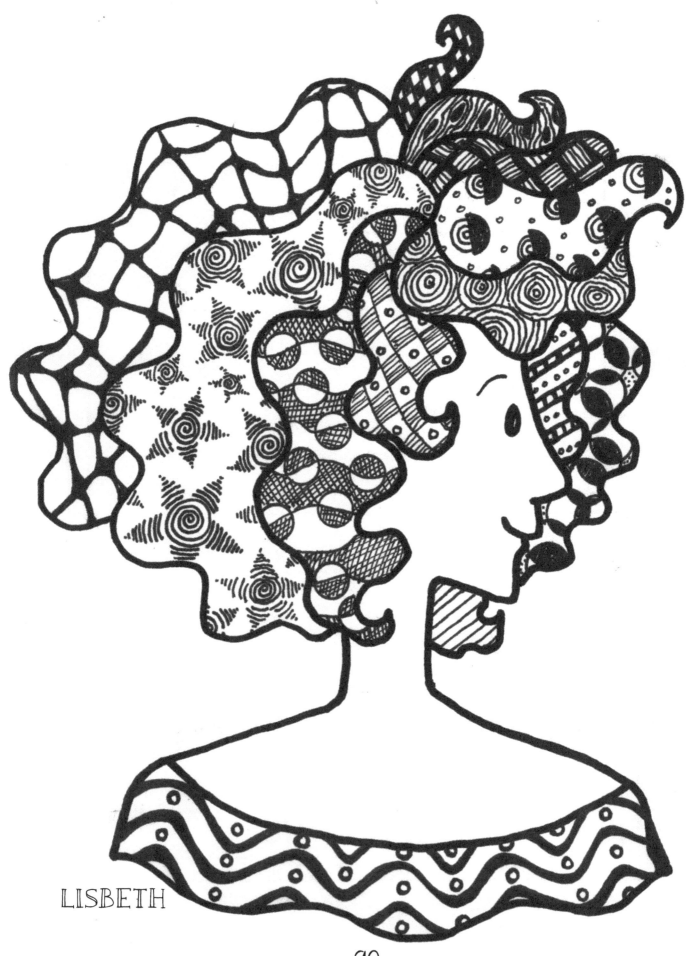

LISBETH

90

THE EASIEST WAY TO BE
CREATIVE: TRY SOMETHING
DIFFERENT, EVEN IF YOU
DON'T THINK IT WILL WORK.

CREATIVESOMETHING.NET

Use a pencil and try to come up with your own doodle patterns.

MARCY

JACQUI

98

> THE BEST USE OF
> IMAGINATION IS CREATIVITY.
> THE WORST USE OF
> IMAGINATION IS ANXIETY.
>
> DEEPAK CHOPRA

HairDoodling ignites your imagination and calms your mind.

> CLEAN OUT A CORNER OF
> YOUR MIND AND
> CREATIVITY WILL
> INSTANTLY FILL IT.
>
> DEE HOCK

HARRIS

102

Use a pencil to practice doodle patterns here.

SARAH

JENNIFER

"YOUR PLAYFUL WAYS ARE A GIFT TO THIS WORLD, SO DON'T BE SHY AND DON'T HOLD BACK."

FLORA BOWLEY
BRAVE INTUITIVE PAINTING
AN ART JOURNAL FOR LIVING CREATIVELY

SAMANTHA

114

Find

HairDoodle
by Heather Tesch

on amazon.com

and

look for more

HairDoodle by Heather Tesch

and other

Doodle by Heather Tesch books

in the future.

All marketing of this book comes from family, friends, and generous readers like you spreading the word.

If you enjoyed

HairDoodle

by Heather Tesch

please consider mentioning it to your friends and followers on social media.

Also consider writing a review on amazon.com

Heather Tesch

Heather Tesch is one of the most loved, trusted, and recognizable faces in television weather. She spent 13 years at The Weather Channel and currently freelances as an on-air meteorologist in Atlanta, Georgia.

Heather loves to draw and doodle, and knows it is a great way to spark creativity in all areas of her life. She has created "HairDoodle by Heather Tesch" to help ignite that same creativity in others.

Heather lives in Atlanta with her husband and two children. Heather is an animal lover, a promoter of pet adoption, and an advocate of spaying and neutering your pets. She shares her home with several adorable critters.

Facebook.com/HeatherTesch.TV
HairDoodle.com

My mom wrote this beautiful story more than 60 years ago when she was in college. She always dreamed of getting it published, but marriage, teaching school, and raising five daughters kept her busy and her dream got set aside. Finally, now in her 80s she decided the time was right - proving it is never too late to go after your dreams.

"The Purple Teddy Bear" is a beautifully illustrated story about a child's Christmas wish and a very special teddy bear. It teaches us to love and embrace the things that make each of us unique.

This is one of the best Christmas stories I have ever read. Yes, I am biased, but it really is a terrific story.

You can help my mom with her dream and purchase "The Purple Teddy Bear" book and a purple teddy at ThePurpleTeddyBear.com and Amazon.com. Many thanks!

REMEMBER, IT IS NEVER TOO LATE TO GO AFTER YOUR DREAMS.